Selection of Prayers
for
Enlightenment

Sixto J. Novaton

blue ocean press
tokyo

Published by:

blue ocean press, an imprint of Aoishima Research Institute
#807-36 Lions Plaza Ebisu
3-25-3 Higashi, Shibuya-ku
Tokyo, Japan 150-0011

Email: contact@blueoceanpublications.com
URL: http://www.blueoceanpublications.com

ISBN: 978-4-902837-22-3

Table of Contents

Afterword How to Elevate a Relative

Introduction

Spirituality is something that needs to be nourished through discipline, dedication, and devotion to ritual. During my early years of serious devotion to spiritual enlightenment, the "I Ching Book of Changes" was very instrumental in spelling out the need for acquiring and strengthening a connection to ancestors, spirit guides, and God. Hence, its 20th oracle in the book (Kuan/Contemplation/View), which stands for strict and true devotion to that which is spiritual and divine. It is the oracle of obtaining spiritual awareness through practice. This practice would yield a connection. At first to ancestors (those closest to us), then other universal divine beings (deities, angels, spiritual protections), in preparedness for entering a higher order of spiritual grace such as priesthood, or shamanistic practice. Otherwise, you would just be a highly graced person without a fully integrated devout purpose. Upon taking your spirituality to the devout level, your spiritual connection and strength is put to the test. Because, its main objective is to serve God by supporting the needs of your family and community.

Here we have a selection of prayer that during my youth enlightened and illuminated me with spiritual grace. These prayers gave me wisdom, and forged a strong connection to all spiritual beings. They lit the flames of passionate spiritual endowment that without I wouldn't be the spiritual being that I am today.

Chapter 1
Traditional Catholic Prayers

Sign of the Cross

In the name of the Father, and of the Son, and of the Holy Spirit
- Amen.

Lord's Prayer

Our Father, who art in heaven, hallowed be thy name;
Thy kingdom come, thy will be done on earth as it is in heaven.
Give us this day our daily bread, and forgive us our trespasses;
As we forgive those who trespass against us, and lead us not into
temptation, but deliver us from evil. Amen.

Hail Mary

Hail Mary, full of grace, the Lord is with you.

Blessed are you among women, and blessed is the fruit of your womb, Jesus.

Holy Mary, Mother of God, pray for us sinners, now and at the hour of our death.

Amen.

Glory Be to the Father

Glory be to the Father, and to the Son, and to the Holy Spirit.
As it was in the beginning, is now, and ever shall be, world
without end.
Amen.

Apostles' Creed

I believe in God, the Father almighty, Creator of heaven and earth, and in Jesus Christ, his only Son, our Lord, who was conceived by the Holy Spirit, born of the Virgin Mary, suffered under Pontius Pilate, was crucified, died and was buried;
He descended into hell, and on the third day he rose again from the dead;
He ascended into heaven, and is seated at the right hand of God the Father almighty;
From there he will come to judge the living and the dead.
I believe in the Holy Spirit, the holy catholic Church, the communion of saints, the forgiveness of sins, the resurrection of the body, and life everlasting. Amen.

Prayer to the Holy Spirit

Come, Holy Spirit, fill the hearts of your faithful. And kindle in them the fire of your love.

Send forth your Spirit and they shall be created. And you will renew the face of the earth.

Lord, by the light of the Holy Spirit you have taught the hearts of your faithful.

In the same Spirit help us to relish what is right and always rejoice in your consolation.

We ask this through Christ our Lord. Amen.

Act of Contrition

My God,

I am sorry for my sins with all my heart.

In choosing to do wrong and failing to do good,

I have sinned against you - whom I should love above all things.

I firmly intend, with your help, to do penance, to sin no more,

And, to avoid whatever leads me to sin.

Our Savior Jesus Christ suffered and died for us.

In his name, my God, have mercy.

Act of Faith

O my God, I firmly believe that you are one God in three divine
Persons, Father, Son, and Holy Spirit. I believe that your divine
Son became man and died for our sins, and that he will come to
judge the living and the dead. I believe these and all the truths
which the holy Catholic Church teaches, because you have
revealed them, who can neither deceive nor be deceived.
Amen.

Act of Hope

O my God, relying on your infinite mercy and promises, I hope to obtain pardon of my sins, the help of your grace, and life everlasting, through the merits of Jesus Christ, my Lord and Redeemer.
Amen.

Act of Love

O my God, I love you above all things with my whole heart and soul, because you are all good and worthy of all my love. I love my neighbor as myself for the love of you. I forgive all who have injured me and I ask pardon of those whom I have injured. Amen.

Guardian Angel Prayer

Angel of God, my guardian dear to whom God's love commits me here;
Ever this day, be at my side to light and guard to rule and guide.
Amen.

Prayer to St. Michael

St. Michael the Archangel, defend us in battle; be our defense against the wickedness and snares of the devil. May God rebuke him, we humbly pray; and do you, O prince of the heavenly host, by the power of God, thrust into hell Satan and the other evil spirits who prowl about the world for the ruin of souls. Amen.

Peace Prayer of Saint Francis

Lord, make me an instrument of your peace:
where there is hatred, let me sow love;
where there is injury, pardon;
where there is doubt, faith;
where there is despair, hope;
where there is darkness, light;
where there is sadness, joy.
O divine Master, grant that I may not so much seek
to be consoled as to console,
to be understood as to understand,
to be loved as to love.
For it is in giving that we receive,
it is in pardoning that we are pardoned,
and it is in dying that we are born to eternal life.
Amen.

Mysteries of the Rosary

The Joyful Mysteries

The Annunciation
Mary learns that she has been chosen to be the mother of Jesus.
The Visitation
Mary visits Elizabeth, who tells her that she will always be remembered.
The Nativity
Jesus is born in a stable in Bethlehem.
The Presentation
Mary and Joseph take the infant Jesus to the Temple to present him to God.
The Finding of Jesus in the Temple
Jesus is found in the Temple discussing his faith with the teachers.

The Mysteries of Light

The Baptism of Jesus in the River Jordan
God proclaims that Jesus is his beloved Son.
The Wedding Feast at Cana
At Mary's request, Jesus performs his first miracle.
The Proclamation of the Kingdom of God
Jesus calls all to conversion and service to the Kingdom.
The Transfiguration of Jesus
Jesus is revealed in glory to Peter, James, and John.

The Institution of the Eucharist
Jesus offers his Body and Blood at the Last Supper.

The Sorrowful Mysteries

The Agony in the Garden
Jesus prays in the Garden of Gethsemane on the night before he dies.
The Scourging at the Pillar
Jesus is lashed with whips.
The Crowning With Thorns
Jesus is mocked and crowned with thorns.
The Carrying of the Cross
Jesus carries the cross that will be used to crucify him.
The Crucifixion
Jesus is nailed to the cross and dies.

The Glorious Mysteries

The Resurrection
God the Father raises Jesus from the dead.
The Ascension
Jesus returns to his Father in heaven.
The Coming of the Holy Spirit
The Holy Spirit comes to bring new life to the disciples.
The Assumption of Mary

At the end of her life on earth, Mary is taken body and soul into heaven.

The Coronation of Mary

Mary is crowned as Queen of Heaven and Earth.

Litany for the Souls of the Departed

Responses are in Italics

In the name of the Father and of the Son, and of the Holy Spirit.
Amen.

Eternal rest give unto them, O Lord,
And let perpetual light shine upon them.

Absolve, O Lord, the souls of the faithful departed from every bond of sin, and by the help of your grace may they be enabled to escape the avenging judgment, and to enjoy the happiness of eternal life.
Amen.

Because in your mercy are deposited the souls that departed in an inferior degree of grace,
Lord have mercy.

Because their present suffering is greatest in the knowledge of the pain that their separation from you is causing you,
Lord have mercy.
Because of their present inability to add to your accidental glory,
Lord have mercy.

Not for our consolation, O Lord; nor for their release from purgative pain, O God; but for your joy and the greater honor of your throne, O Christ the King,
Lord have mercy.

For the souls of our departed friends, relatives and benefactors,
Grant light and peace, O Lord.

For those of our family who have fallen asleep in Thy bosom, O Jesus,
Grant light and peace, O Lord.

For those who have gone to prepare our place,
Grant light and peace, O Lord.

For priests who were our spiritual directors,
Grant light and peace, O Lord.

For men or women who were our teachers in school,
Grant light and peace, O Lord.

For those who were our employers or employees,
Grant light and peace, O Lord.

For those who were our associates in daily toil,
Grant light and peace, O Lord.
For any soul whom we ever offended,
Grant light and peace, O Lord.

For our enemies now departed,
Grant light and peace, O Lord.

For those souls who have none to pray for them,

Grant light and peace, O Lord.

For those forgotten by their friends and relatives,
Grant light and peace, O Lord.

For those now suffering the most,
Grant light and peace, O Lord.

For those who, while on earth, were most devoted to God the Holy Ghost, and to the holy Mother of God,
Grant light and peace, O Lord.

For all deceased bishops and prelates,
Grant light and peace, O Lord.

For all deceased priests, seminarians and religious,
Grant light and peace, O Lord.

For all our brethren in the Faith everywhere,
Grant light and peace, O Lord.

For all our separated brethren who deeply loved Thee, and would have come into Thy household had they known the truth,
Grant light and peace, O Lord.

For those souls who need our prayers,
Grant light and peace, O Lord.

For those, closer to you than we are, whose prayers we need,
Grant light and peace, O Lord.

That those may be happy with you forever, who on earth were true exemplars of the Orthodox Catholic Faith,
Grant them eternal rest, O Lord.

That those may be admitted to your unveiled Presence, who as far as we know never committed mortal sin,
Grant them eternal rest, O Lord.

That those may be housed in glory, who lived always in recollection and prayer,
Grant them eternal rest, O Lord.

That those may be given the celestial joy of beholding you, who lived lives of mortification, self-denial, and penance,
Grant them eternal rest, O Lord.

That those may be flooded with your love, who denied themselves even your favors of indulgence and who made the heroic act for the souls who had gone before them,

Grant them eternal rest, O Lord.

That those may be drawn up to the Beatific Vision, who never put obstacles in the way of sanctifying grace and who ever drew closer in mystical union with you,
Grant them eternal rest O Lord.

We most especially pray for _____ that you will grant them eternal rest O Lord.

And let perpetual light shine upon them.

Our Father.....

Note: **Readings from the Rites of Burial or from the Funeral Liturgy may be read here, followed by a homily or sermon, if this devotion takes place as a service unto itself. If this devotion precedes or follows Mass or one of the Hours, the readings and sermon are omitted.**

Let us pray: Be mindful, O Lord, of all your servants and handmaids who are gone before us with the sign of faith and repose in the sleep of grace. To these, O Lord, and to all who rest in Christ, grant, we beseech you, a place of refreshment, light and peace, through the same Christ Our Lord. *Amen.*

Prayer for the Forgotten Dead

O merciful God, take pity on those souls who have no particular friends and intercessors to recommend them to you, who, either through the negligence of those who are alive, or through length of time are forgotten by their friends and by all. Spare them, O Lord, and remember Your own mercy, when others forget to appeal to it. Let not the souls which you have created be parted from you, their Creator, through our Lord Jesus Christ, your Son who lives and reign with you and the Holy Spirit, One God, unto the ages of ages. Amen.

May the souls of all the faithful departed, through the mercy of God, rest in peace. Amen.

Chapter 2
Dead Sea Scrolls

Hymn 11

I thank Thee, O Lord, for Thou hast upheld me by Thy strength. Thou hast shed Thy Holy Spirit upon me that L may not stumble. Thou host strengthen me before the battles of wickedness, and during all their disasters. Thou hast not permitted that fear should cause me to desert Thy Covenant. Thou hast made me like a strong tower, a high wall, and hast established my edifice upon rock; eternal foundations serve for my ground, and all my ramparts are a tried wall which shall not sway. Thou hast placed me, O my God, among the branches of the Council of holiness; Thu hast {established mu mouth} in Thy Covenant, and my tongue is like that of Thy disciples; whereas the spirit of disaster is without a mouth and all the sons of iniquity without a reply; for the lying lips shall be Judgment all those who assail me, distinguishing through me between the just and the wicked. For Thou knowest the whole intent of a creature, Thou discernest every reply, and Thou hast established my heart [on] Thy teaching and truth, directing my steps into the paths of righteousness that I may walk before Thee in the land [of the living], into paths of glory and [infinite] peace which shall [never] end. For thou knowest the inclination of Thy servant, that I have not relied [upon the works of my hands] to raise up [my heart], nor have I sought refuge in my own strength. I have no fleshly refuge, [and Thy servant has] no righteous deeds, to deliver him from the [Pit of no] forgiveness. But I lean on the [abundance of Thy mercies] and hope [for the greatness] of Thy grace, that Thou wilt bring [salvation] to flower and the branch to growth, providing refuge in (Thy) strength [and raising up my heart]. [For in] Thy righteous Thou hast appointed me Thy Covenant, and I have clung to Thy truth and [gone forward in Thy ways].Thou hast made me a father to the sons of grace, and as a foster-father to men of marvel; they have opened their mouths like little babes... like a child playing in the lap of its nurse. Thou hast lifted my horn above those who insult me, and those who attack me [swag like the boughs] (of a tree); my enemies are like chaff before the wind, and my dominion is over the sons [of iniquity, For] Thou hast succoured mu soul, O my God, and hast lifted my horn on high. And I shall shine in a seven-fold light in [the Council appointed by] Thee for Thy glory; for Thou art an everlasting heavenly light to me and wilt establish my feet [upon level ground for ever]

Hymn 12

I thank Thee, O Lord, for Thou hast enlightened me though Thy truth. In Thy marvelous mysteries, and in Thy lovingkindness to a man [of vanity, and] in the greatness of Thy mercy to a perverse heart Thou hast granted me knowledge. Who is like Thee among the gods, O lord, and who is according Thy truth? Who, when he judged, shall be righteous before Thee? For no spirit can reply to Thy rebuke nor can any withstand Thy wrath. Yet Thou bringest all the sons of Thy truth in forgiveness before Thee, [to cleanse] them of their faults through Thy great goodness, and to establish them before Thee through the multitude of Thy mercies for ever and ever. For Thou art an eternal God; all Thy ways are determined for ever [and ever] and there is none other beside Thee. And what is a man of Naughty and Vanity that he should understand Thy marvelous mighty deeds?

Hymn 15

I thank Thee, O Lord, and nothing exists except by Thy will; none can consider [Thy deep secrets] or contemplate Thy [mysteries]. What then is man that is earth, that shaped [from clay] and return to the dust, that Thou shouldst gave him to understand such marvels and make knows to him the counsel of [Thy truth]? Clay and dust that I am, what can I devise unless Thou wish it, and what contrive unless Thou desire it? What strength shall I have unless Thou keep me upright, and how shall I understand unless by (the spirits) which Thou hast shaped for me? What can I say unless Thou open my mouth and how can I answer unless Thou enlighten me? Behold, Thou art Prince of gods and King of majesties, Lord of all spirits, Ruler of all creatures; nothing is done without Thee, and nothing is known without Thy will. Beside Thee there is nothing, and nothing can compare with Thee is strength; in the presence of Thy glory there is nothing, and Thy might is without price. Who among Thy great and marvellous creature can stand in the presence of Thy glory? How then can he who returns to his dust? For Thy glory's sake alone hast Thou made all these things.

Hymn 19

I will praise Thy Name among them that fear Thee. Bowing down in prayer I will beg thy favours [From generation to generation] and from season to season without end: When light emerges from [Its dwelling-place], and when the day reaches it appointed end in accordance with the laws of the Great Light of heaven; when evening falls and light departs at the beginning of the dominion of darkness, at the hour appointed for night, and at its end when morning returns and (the shadows) retire to their dwelling-place before the approach of light; always, at the genesis of every period and at the beginning of every age and at the end of every seasons, according to the statute and signs appointed to every dominion by the certain law from the mouth of God, by the precept which is and shall be for ever and ever without end. Without it nothing is nor shall be, for the God of knowledge established it and there is no other beside Him. I, the Master know Thee O my God, by the spirit which Thou hast given to me, and by Thy Holy Spirit I have faithfully hearkened to Thy marvellous counsel. In the mystery of Thy wisdom Thou hast opended knowledge to me, and in Thy mercies [Thou hast unlock for me] the fountain of Thy might ... Before Thee no man is just... [that he may] understand all Thy mysteries or give answer [to Thy rebuke. But the children of Thy grace shall delight in] Thy correction and watch for Thy goodness, for in Thy mercies [Thou wilt show Thyself to them] and they shall know Thee; at the time of Thy glory they shall rejoice. [Thou hast caused them to draw near] in accordance [with their knowledge], and hast admitted them in accordance with their understanding, and in their divisions they shall serve Thee throughout their dominion [without ever turning aside] from Thee or transgressing Thy word. Behold, [I was taken] from dust [and] fashioned [out of clay] as a source of uncleanness, and a shameful nakedness, a heap dust, and a kneading [with water,]... and a house of darkness, a creature of clay returning to dust, returning [at the appointed time to dwell] in the dust whence it was taken. How then shall dust reply [to its Maker, and how] understand His [work]? How shall it stand before Him who reproves it?... [and the Springs of] Eternity, the Well of Glory and the Fountain of Knowledge. Not even [the wonderful] Heroes [can] declare all Thy glory or stand in face of Thy wrath, and there is none among them that can answer Thy rebuke; for Thou art just and none can oppose Thee. How then can (man) who returns to his dust? I hold my peace; what more shall I say than this? I have spoken in accordance with my knowledge, out of the righteousness given to a creature of clay. And how shall I speak unless Thou open my mouth; how understand unless Thou teach me? How shall I seek Thee unless Thou uncover my heart, and how follow the way that is straight unless [Thou guide me? How shall my foot] stay on [the path unless Thou] give it strength; and how shall I rise...

Hymn 20

All these things [Thou didst established in Thy wisdom. Thou didst appoint] all Thy works before ever creating them: the host of Thy spirits and Congregations [of Thy Holy Ones, and heavens and all] their hosts and the earth and all it bring forth. In the seas and deeps... and an everlasting task; for Thou hast established them from before eternity. And the work of... and they shall recount Thy glory throughout all Thy dominion. For Thou hast shown them that which they had not [seen by removing all] ancient things and creating new ones, by breaking asunder things anciently established, and raising up the things of eternity. For [Thou art from the beginning] and shalt endure for ages without end. And Thou hast [appointed] all these things in the mysteries of Thy wisdom to make known Thy glory [to all]. [But what is] the spirit of flesh that it should understand all this, and that it should comprehend the great [design of Thy wisdom]? What is he that is born of woman in the midst of all Thy terrible [works]? He is but an edifice of dust, and a thing kneaded with water, whose beginning [is sinful iniquity], and shameful nakedness, [and a fount of uncleanness], and over whom a spirit of straying rules. If he is wicked he shall become [a sign for] ever, and a wonder to [every] generation, and an object of horror to all flesh. By Thy goodness alone is man righteous, and with Thy many mercies [Thou strengthenest him]. Thou wilt adorn him with Thy splendour and wilt [cause him to reign amid] many delights with everlasting peace and length of days. [For Thou hast spoken], and Thou wilt not take back Thy word. And I, Thy servant, I know by the spirit which Thou hast given to me [that

Thy words are truth], and that all Thy works are righteousness and that Thou wilt not take back Thy word...

Hymn 21

[Blessed art Thou, O lord, who hast given understanding to the heart of [Thy] servant that he may... and resist [the works] of wickedness and blew [Thy Name always, and that he may choose all] that Thou lovest and loathe all that Thou [hatest]... [For Thou hast divided men] into good and evil in accordance with the spirits of their lot; [in accordance with] their [divisions do they accomplished] their task. And I know through the understanding which come from Thee, that in Thy goodwill towards [ashes Thou hast shed] Thy Holy Spirit [upon me] and thus drawn me near to understanding of Thee. And the closer I approach, the more am I filled with zeal against all the workers of iniquity and the men of deceit. For none of those who approach Thee rebels against Thy command, nor do any of those who know Thee alter Thy words; for Thou art just, and all Thine elect are truth. Thou wilt blot out all wickedness [and sin] for ever, and Thy righteousness shall be revealed before the eyes of all Thy creatures. I know through Thy great goodness; and with an oath I have undertaken never to sin against Thee, nor to do anything evil in Thine eyes. And thus do I bring into community all the men of my Council. I will cause each man to draw near in accordance with his understanding, and according to the greatness of his portion so will I love him. I will not honour an evil man, nor consider [the bribes of the wicked]; I will [not] barter Thy truth for riches, nor one of Thy precepts for bribes. But according as [Thou drawest a man near to Thee, so will I love] him, and according as Thou removest him far from Thee, so

will I hate him; and none of those who have turned [from] Thy
[Covenant] will I bring into the Council [of Thy truth].

Hymn 22

I thank Thee, O Lord, as befits the greatness of Thy power and the multitude of Thy marvels for ever and ever. [Thou art merciful God] and rich in [favours], pardoning those who repent of their sin and visiting the iniquity of the wicked. [Thou delightest in] the free-will offering [of the righteous] but iniquity Thou hatest always. Thou hast favoured me, Thy servant, with spirit of knowledge, [that I may choose] truth [and goodness] and loathe all the ways of iniquity. And I have loved Thee freely and with all my heart; [contemplating the mysteries of] Thy wisdom [I have sought Thee] For this is from Thy hand and [nothing is done] without [Thy will]. I have loved Thee freely and with all my heart and soul. I have purified... [that I might not] turn aside from any of Thy commands. I have clung to the Congregation... that I might not be separated from any Thy laws. I know through the understanding which comes from Thee that righteousness is not in a hand of flesh, [that] man [is not master of] his way and that it is not in mortals to direct their step. I know that the inclination of every spirit [is in Thy hand]; Thou didst established [all] its [ways] before ever creating it, and how can any man change Thy words? Thou alone didst [create] the just and establish him from the womb for the time of goodwill, that he might hearken to Thy Covenant and walk in all (Thy ways), and that [Thou mightiest show Thyself great] to him in the multitude of Thy mercies, and enlarge his straitened soul to eternal salvation, to perpetual and unfailing peace. Thou wilt raise up his glory from among flesh. But the wicked Thou didst create for [the time] of Thy [wrath], Thou didst vow them from

41

the womb to the Day of Massacre, for they walk in the way which is not good. They have despised [Thy Covenant] and their souls have loathed Thy [truth]; they have taken no delight in all Thy commandments and have chosen that which Thou hatest. [For according to the mysteries] of Thy [wisdom], Thou hast ordained them for great chastisements before the eyes of all Thy creatures, that [for all] eternity they may serve as sign [and a wonder], and that [all men] may know Thy glory and Thy tremendous power. But what is flesh that it should understand [these things]? And how should [a creature of] dust his steps? It is Thou who didst shape the spirit and establish its work [from the beginning]; the way of all the living proceeds from Thee. I know that no riches equal Thy truth, and [have therefore desired to enter the Council of] Thy holiness. I know that Thou hast chosen them before all others and that they shall serve Thee for ever. Thou wilt [take no bribe for the deeds of iniquity], nor ransom for the works of wickedness; for Thou art a God of truth and [wilt destroy] all iniquity [for ever, and] no [wickedness shall exist before Thee.

Because I know all these things my tongue shall utter a reply. Bowing down and [confessing all] my transgressions, I will seek [Thy] spirits [of knowledge]; cleaving to Thy spirit of [holiness], I will hold fast to the truth of Thy Covenant, the [I may serve] Thee in truth and wholeness of heart, and that I may love [Thy Name]. Blessed art Thou, O Lord, Maker [of all things and mighty in] deeds: all things are Thy work! Behold, Thou art pleased to favour [Thy servants], and hast graced me with Thy spirits of mercy and [with the radiance] of Thy glory. Thine, Thine is righteousness, for it is Thou who hast done all [these things]! I know that Thou hast marked the spirit of the just, and therefore I have chosen to keep my hands clean in accordance with [Thy] will; the soul of Thy servant [has loathed] every work of iniquity.

And I know that man is not righteous except through Thee, by the spirit which Thou hast given [me] to perfect Thy [favours] to Thy servant [for ever], purifying me by Thy Holy Spirit, and drawing me near Thee by Thy grace according to the abundance of Thy mercies... [Grant me] the place [of Thy lovingkindness] which [Thou hast] chosen for them that love Thee and keep [Thy commandments, that they may stand] in Thy presence [for] ever.... Let no scourge [come] near him lest he stagger aside from the laws of Thy Covenant.... I [know, O Lord that Thou art merciful] and compassionate, [long]-suffering and [rich] in grace and truth, pardoning transgression [and sin]. Thou repentest of [evil against them that love Thee] and keep [Thy] commandments, [that] return to Thee with faith and wholeness of heart... to serve Thee [and to do that what is] good in Thine eyes. Reject not the face of Thy servant ....

Chapter 3
Book of Psalms

Psalm 1

Blessed is the man that walketh not in the counsel of the ungodly, nor standeth in the way of sinners, nor sitteth in the seat of the scornful. 2- But his delight is in the law of the lord; and in the law doth he meditate day and night. 3- And he shall be like a tree planted by the rivers of the water, that bringeth forth his fruit in his season; his leaf also shall not wither; and whatsoever he doeth shall prosper. 4- The ungodly are not so; but are liker the chaff which the wind driveth away. 5- Therefore the ungodly shall not stand in judgment, nor sinners in congregation of the righteous. 6- For the Lord knoweth the way of the righteous: but the way o the ungodly shall perish.

Psalm 8

O Lord our Lord, how excellent is thy name in all the earth! Who hast set thy glory above the heavens. 2- Out of the mouth of babes and sucklings hast thou ordained strength because of thine enemies, that thou mightiest still the enemy and the avengers. 3- When I consider thy heavens, the work of thy fingers, the moon and the stars, which thou hast ordained; 4- What is man, that thou art mindful of him? 5- For thou hast made him a little lower than the angels, and hast crowned him with glory and honour. 6- Thou madest him to have dominion over the works of thy hands; thou hast put all things under his feet: 7- All sheep and oxen, yea and the beasts of the field; 8- The fowl of the air, and the fish of the sea, and whatsoever passeth through the paths of the seas. 9- O Lord our Lord, how excellent is thy name in all the earth!

Psalm 11

In the Lord put I my trust: how say ye to my soul, Flee as a bird to your mountain? 2- For, lo, the wicked bend their bow, they make ready their arrow upon the string, that they may privily shoot at the upright in heart. 3-If the foundation be destroyed, what can the righteous do? 4-The Lord is in my holy temple, the Lord's throne is in heaven: his eyes behold, his eyelids try, the children of men. 5- The Lord trieth the righteous: but the wicked and him that loveth violence his soul hateth. 6- Upon the wicked he shall rain snares, fire and brimstone, and an horrible tempest: this shall be the portion of their cup. 7- For the righteousness Lord loveth countenance doth behold the upright.

Psalm 13- How long wilt thou forget me, O Lord? For ever? How long wilt thou hide thy face from me? 2- How long shall I take counsel in my soul, having sorrow in my heart daily? How long shall my enemy be exalted over me? 3- Consider and hear me, O Lord my God, lighten mine eyes, lest I sleep the sleep of death; 4-Lest my enemy say, I have prevailed against him; and those that trouble me rejoice when I am moved. 5- But I have trusted in thy mercy; my heart shall rejoice in thy salvation. 6- I will sing unto the Lord, because he hath dealt bountifully with me.

Psalm 14

The fool hath said in his heart, there is no God. They are corrupt, they have done abominable works, there is none that doeth good. 2- The Lord looked down upon the children of men, to see if there were any that did understand, and seek God. 3- They are all gone aside, they are all together become filthy: there is none doeth good, no, not one. 4- Have all the workers of iniquity no knowledge? Who eats up my people as they eat bread, and call not upon the Lord. 5- There were they in great fear: for God is in the generation of the righteous. 6- Ye have shamed the counsel of the poor, because the Lord is his refuge. 7- Oh that the salvation of Israel were come out of Zion! When the Lord bringeth back the captivity of his people, Jacob shall rejoice, and Israel shall be glad.

Psalm 17

Hear the right, O Lord, attend unto my cry, give ear unto, my prayer, that goeth not out of feigned lips. 2- Let my sentence come forth from thy presence; let thine eyes behold the things that are equal. 3- Thou has proved my heart; thou hast visited me in the night; thou hast tried me, and shalt find nothing; I am purposed that my mouth shall not transgress. 4- Concerning the works of men, by the word of thy lips I have kept me from the paths of the destroyer. 5- Hold up my goings in thy paths, that my footsteps slip not. 6- I have called upon thee, for thou wilt hear me, O God: incline thine ear unto me, and hear my speech. 7- Shew thy marvelous lovingkindness, O thou that savest by thy right hand them which put their trust in thee from those that rise up against them. 8- Keep me as the apple of the eye, hide me under the shadow of thy wings. 9- From the wicked that oppress me, from my deadly enemies, who compass me about. 10- They are inclosed in their own fat: with their mouth they speak proudly. 11- They have now compassed us in our steps: they have set their eyes bowing down to the earth; 12- Like as a lion that is greedy of his prey, and as it were young lion lurking in secret places. 13- Arise, O Lord, disappoint him, cast him down: deliver my soul from the wicked, which thy sword: 14- From men which are thy hand, O Lord, from men of the world, which have their portion in this life, and whose belly thou fillest with thy hid treasure: they are full of children, and leave he rest of their substance to their babes. 15- As for me, I will behold thy face in righteous: I shall be satisfied, when I awake, with thy likeness.

Psalm 18

I will love thee, O Lord, my strength. 2- The Lord is my rock, and my fortress, and my deliverer; my God, my strength, in whom I will trust; my buckler, and the horn of my salvation, and my high tower. 3- I will call upon the Lord, who is worthy to be praised: so shall I be saved from mine enemies. 4- The sorrow of death compassed me, and the floods of ungodly men made me afraid. 5- The sorrow of hell compassed me about: the snares of death prevented me. 6- In my distress I called upon the Lord; and cried unto my God: he heard my voice out of his temple, and my cry came before him, even into his ears. 7- Then the earth shook and trembled; the foundation also of the hills moved and were shaken, because he was wroth. 8- There went up a smoke out of his nostrils, and fire out of his mouth devoured: coals were kindled by it. 9- He bowed the heavens also, and came down: and darkness was under his feet. 10- And he rode upon a cherub, and did fly: yea, he did fly upon the wings of the wind. 11- He made darkness his secret place; his pavilion round about him were dark waters and thick clouds of the skies. 12- At the brightness that was before him his thick clouds passed, hail stones and coal of fire. 13- The Lord also thundered in the heavens, and the highest gave his voice; hail stones and coal of fire. 14- Yea, he sent out his arrows, and scattered them; and he shot out lightening, and discomfited them. 15- Then the channels of waters were seen, and the foundation of the world were discovered at rebuke, O Lord at the blast of the breath of thy nostrils. 16- He sent from above, he took me, he drew me out of many waters. 17- He delivered me from my strong enemy, and from them which hated me: for they were too strong for me. 18- They prevented me in the day of my calamity but the Lord was my stay. 19- He brought me forth also into a large place; he delivered me, because he delighted in me. 20- The Lord rewarded me according to my righteousness; according to the cleanness of my hands hath he recompensed me. 21- For I have kept the ways of the Lord, and have not wickedly departed from my God. 22- For all his judgments were before me, and I did not put away his statutes from me. 23- I was also upright before him, and I kept myself from mine iniquity. 24- Therefore hath the Lord recompensed me according to my righteousness, according to the cleanness of my hands in his eyesight. 25- With the merciful thou wit shew thyself merciful; with an upright man thou wilt shew thyself upright; 26- With the pure thou wilt shew thyself pure; and with the froward thou wilt shew thyself forward. 27- For thou wilt save the afflicted people: but wilt bring down high looks. 28- For thou wilt light my candles: the Lord my God will enlighten my darkness. 29- For by thee I have run through a troop; and by my God have I leaped over a wall. 30- As for God, his way is perfect: the word of the Lord is tried: he is a buckler to all those that trust in him. 31- For who is God save the Lord? Or who is a rock save our God? 32- It is God that girdeth me with strength, and market my way perfect. 33- He maketh my feet like hinds' feet, and setteth me upon my high places. 34- He teacheth my hands to war, so that a bow of steel is broken by mine arms. 35- Thou hast also given me the shield of thy salvation: and thy right hand hath holden me up, and thy gentleness hath made me great. 36- Thou hast enlarged my steps under me, that my feet did not slip. 37- I have pursue mine enemies, and overtaken them: neither did I turn again till they were consumed. 38- I have wounded them that they were not able to rise; they are fallen under my feet. 39- For thou hast girded me with strength unto battle: thou hast subdued under me those that rose up against me. 40- Those hast also given me the necks of mine enemies; that I might destroy them that hate me. 41- They cried, but there was none to save them: even unto the Lord, but he answered them not. 42- Then did I beat them small as the dust before the wind; I did cast them out as the dirt in the streets. 43- Thou hast delivered me from the strivings of the people; and thou hast made me the head of the hearthen: a people whom I have not known shall serve me. 44- As soon as they hear of me, they shall obey me: the strangers shall submit themselves unto me. 45- The strangers shall fade away, and be afraid out of their close places. 46- The Lord liveth; and blessed be my rock; and let the God of my salvation be exalted. 47- It is God that avengeth me, and subdueth the people under me. 48- He delivereth me from mine enemies: yea, thou liftest me up above those that rise up against: thou hast delivered me from the violent man. 49- Therefore will I give thanks unto thee, O Lord, among the heathen, and sing praises unto thy name. 50- Great deliverance giveth he to his king; and sheweth mercy to his anointed, to David, and to his seed for evermore.

Psalm 19

The heavens declare the glory of God; and the firmament sheweth his handywork. 2- Day unto day uttereth speech, and night unto night sheweth knowledge. 3- There is no speech nor language, where their voice is not heard. 4- Their line is gone out through all the earth, and their words to the end of the world. In them hath he set a tabernacle for the sun. 5- Which is as a bridegroom coming out of his chamber, and rejoiceth as a strong man to run a race. 6- His going forth is from the end of the heavens, and his circuit unto the ends of it: and there is nothing hid from the heat thereof. 7- The law of the Lord is perfect, converting the soul: the testimony of the Lord is sure, making wise the simple. 8- The statues of the Lord are right, rejoicing the heart: the commandment of the Lord is pure, enlightening the eyes. 9- The fear of the Lord is clean, enduring for ever: the judgments of the Lord are true and righteous altogether. 10- More to be desired are they than gold, yea, than much fine gold: sweeter also than honey and the honeycomb. 11- Moreover by them is thy servant warned: and in keeping of them there is great reward. 12- Who can understand his errors? Cleanse thou me from secret faults. 13- Keep back thy servant also from presumptuous sins; let them not have dominion over me: then shall I be upright, and I shall be innocent from the great transgression. 14- Let the words of my mouth, and the meditation of my heart, be acceptable in thy sight, O Lord, my strength, and my redeemer.

Psalm 20

The Lord hear thee in the day of trouble; the name of the God of Jacob defend thee; 2- Send thee help from the sanctuary, and strengthen thee out of Zion; 3- Remember all thy offerings, and accept thy burnt sacrifice; Se-lah. 4- Grant thee according to thine own heart, and fulfil all thy counsel. 5- We will rejoice in thy salvation, and in thy name God we will set up our banners; the Lord fulfil all thy petitions. 6- Now know I that the Lord saveth his anointed; he will hear him from his body heavens with the saving strength of his right hand. 7- Some trust in chariots, and some in horses: but we will remember the name of the Lord our God. 8- They are brought down and fallen: but we are risen, and stand upright. 9- Save, Lord: let the king hear us when we call.

Psalm 22

My God, my God, why hast thou forsaken me? Why art thou so far from helping me, and from the words of my roaring? 2- O my God, I cry in the daytime, but thou hearest not; and in the night season, and am not silent. 3- But thou art holy, O thou that inhabitest the praises of Israel. 4- Our father trusted in thee; they trusted, and thou didst deliver them. 5- They cried unto thee, and were delivered: they trusted in thee, and were not confounded. 6- But I am a worm, and no man; a reproach of men, and despised of the people. 7- All they that see me laugh me to scorn: they shoot out the lip, they shake the head, saying, 8- He trusted on the Lord that he would deliver him: let him deliver him, seeing he delighted in him. 9- But thou art he that took me out of the womb: thou didst make me hope when I was upon my mother's breasts. 10- I was cast upon thee from the womb: thou art my God from my mother's belly. 11- Be not far from me; for trouble is near; for there is none to help. 12- Many bulls have compassed me: strong bulls of Ba-shan have beset me round. 13- They gaped upon me with their mouths, as a ravening and a roaring lion. 14- I am poured out like water, and all my bones are out of joint: my heart is like wax; it is melted in the midst of my bowels. 15- My strength is dried up like a potsherd; and my tongue cleaveth to my jaws; and thou hast brought me into the dust of death. 16- For dogs have compassed me: the assembly of the wicked have inclosed me: they pierced my hands and my feet. 17- I may tell all my bones: they look and stare upon me. 18- They part my garments among them, and cast lots upon my vesture. 19- But be not thou far from me, O Lord; O my strength, haste thee to help me. 20- Deliver my soul from the sword; my darling from the power of the dog. 21- Save me from the lion's mouth: for thou hast heard me from the horns of the unicorns. 22- I will declare thy name unto my brethren: in the midst of congregation will I praise thee. 23- Ye that fear the Lord, praise him; all ye the seed of Jacob, gloryify him; and fear him, all ye the seed of Israel. 24- For he hath not despised nor abhorred the affliction of the afflicted; neither hath he hid his face from him; but when he cried unto him, he heard. 25- My praise shall be of thee in the great congregation: I will pay my vows before them that fear him. 26- The meek shall eat and be satisfied: they shall praise the Lord that seek him: your heart shall live for ever. 27- All the ends of the world shall remember and turn unto the Lord: and all the kindreds of the nations shall worship before thee. 28- For the kingdom is the Lord's: and he is the governor among the nations. 29- All they that be fat upon earth shall eat and worship: all they that go down to the dust shall bow before him; and none can keep alive his own soul. 30- A seed shall serve him; it shall be accounted to the Lord for a generation. 31- They shall come, and shall declare his righteousness unto a people that shall be born, that he hath done this.

Psalm 23

The Lord is my shepherd; I shall not want. 2- He maketh me to lie down in green pastures: he leadeth me beside the still waters. 3- He restoreth my soul: he leadeth me in the paths of righteousness his is name's sake. 4- Yea, though I walk through the valley of the shadow of death, I will fear no evil: for thou art with me; thy rod and thy staff they comfort me. 5- Thou preparest a table before me in the presence of mine enemies: thou anointest my head with oil; my cup runneth over. 6- Surly goodness and mercy shall follow me all the days of my life: and I will dwell in the house of the Lord for ever.

Psalm 24

The earth is the Lord's and the fullness thereof; the world, and they that dwell therein. 2- For he hath founded it upon the seas, and established it upon the floods. 3- Who shall ascend into the hill of the Lord? Or who shall stand in his holy place? 4- He that hath clean hands, and a pure heart; who hath not lifted up his soul unto vanity, nor sworn deceitfully. 5- He shall receive the blessing from the Lord, and righteousness from the God of his salvation. 6- This is the generation of them that seek him, that seek thy face, O Jacob. Se-lah. 7- Lifted up your heads, O ye gates; and be ye lifted up, ye everlasting doors; and the King of glory shall come in. 8- Who is the King of the glory? The Lord strong and mighty, the Lord mighty in battle. 9- Lift up our heads, O ye gates; even lift them up, ye everlasting doors; and the King of the glory shall come in. 10- Who is this King of glory? The Lord of hosts, he is the King of glory. Se-lah.

Psalm 25

Unto thee, O Lord, do I lift up my soul, 2- O my God, I trust in thee: let me not be ashamed, let me not mine enemies triumph over me. 3- Yea, let none that wait on thee be ashamed: let them be ashamed which transgress without cause. 4- Shew me thy ways, O Lord; teach me thy paths. 5- Lead me in thy truth, and teach me: for thou art the God of my salvation; on thee do I wait all the day. 6- Remember, O Lord thy tender mercies and thy loveingkindnesses; for they have been ever of old. 7- Remember not the sins of my youth, nor my transgressions: according to thy mercy remember thou me for thy goodness sake, O Lord. 8- Good and upright is the Lord: therefore will he teach sinners in the way. 9- The meek will he guide in judgment: and the meek will he teach his way. 10- All the paths of the Lord are mercy and truth unto such as keep his covenant and his testimonies. 11- For thy name's sake, O Lord, pardon mine iniquity; for it is great. 12- What man is he that feareth the Lord? Him shall he teach in the way that he shall choose. 13- His soul shall dwell at ease; and his seed shall inherit the earth. 14- The secret of the Lord is with them that fear him; and he will shew them his covenant. 15- Mine eyes are ever toward the Lord; for he shall pluck my feet out of the net. 16- Turn thee unto me, and have mercy upon me; for I am desolate and afflicted. 17- The trouble of my heart are enlarged: O bring thou me out of my distresses. 18- Look upon mine affliction and my pain; and forgive all my sins. 19- Consider mine enemies; for they are many; and they hate me with cruel hatred. 20- O keep my soul, and deliver me: let me not be ashamed; for I put my trust in thee. 21- Let integrity and

uprightness preserve me; for I wait on thee. 22- Redeem Israel, O
God, out of all his troubles.

Psalm 26

Judge me, O Lord; for I have walked in mine integrity; I have trusted also in the Lord; therefore I shall not slide. 2- Examine me, O Lord, and prove me; try my reins and my heart. 3- For thy lovingkindness is before mine eyes: and I have walked in thy truth. 4- I have not sat with vain persons, neither will I go in with dissemblers. 5- I have hated the congregation of evil doers; and will not sit with the wicked. 6- I will wash mine hands in innocency: so will I compass thine altar, O Lord: 7- That I may publish with the voice of thanksgiving, and tell of all thy wondrous works. 8- Lord, I have loved the habitation of thy house, and the place where thine honour dwelleth. 9- Gather not my soul with sinners, nor my life with bloody men: 10- In whose hands is mischief, and their right hands is full of bribes. 11- But as for me, I will walk in mine integrity: redeem me, and be merciful unto me. 12- My foot standeth in an even place: in the congregations will I bless the Lord.

Psalm 27

The Lord is my light and my salvation; whom shall I fear? The Lord is the strength of my life; of whom shall I be afraid? 2- When the wicked even mine enemies and my foes, came upon me to eat up my flesh, they stumbled and fell. 3- Though an host should encamp against me, my heart shall not fear: though was should rise against me, in this will I be confident. 4- One thing have I desired of the Lord, that will I seek after; that I may dwell in the house of the Lord all the days of my life, to behold the beauty of the Lord, and to inquire in his temple. 5- For in the time of trouble he shall hide me in his pavilion: in the secret of his tabernacle shall he hide me; he shall set me up upon a rock. 6- And now shall mine head be lifted up above mine enemies round about me: therefore will I offer in his tabernacle sacrifices of joy; I will sing, yea, I will sing praises unto the Lord. 7- Hear, O Lord, when I cry with my voice: have mercy also upon me, and answer me. 8- When thou sadist, Seek ye my face; my heart said unto thee, Thy face, Lord, will I seek. 9- Hide not thy face far from me; put not thy servant away in anger: thou hast been my help; leave me not, neither forsake me, O God of my salvation. 10- When my father and my mother forsake me, then the Lord will take me up. 11- Teach me thy way, O Lord, and lead me in a plain path, because of mine enemies. 12- Deliver me not over unto the will of mine enemies; for false witnesses are risen up against me, and such as breathe out cruelty. 13- I had fainter, unless I had believed to see the goodness of the Lord in the land of the living. 14- Wait on the Lord: be of good courage, and he shall strengthen thine heart; wait. I say, on the Lord.

Psalm 28

Unto thee will I cry, O Lord my rock; be not silent to me: lest, if thou be silent to me, I become like them that go down into the pit. 2- Hear the voice of my supplications, when I cry unto thee, when I lifted up my hands toward thy holy oracle. 3- Draw me not away with the wicked, and with the workers, of iniquity, which speak peace to their neighbours, but mischief is in their hearts. 4- Give them according to their deeds, and according to the wickedness of their endeavours: give them after the work of their hands; render to them their desert. 5- Because they regard not the works of the Lord, nor the operation of his hands, he shall destroy them, and not build them up. 6- Blessing be the Lord, because he hath heard the voice of my supplications. 7- The Lord is my strength and my shield; my heart trusted in him, and I am helped: therefore my heart greatly rejoiceth: and with my song will I praise him. 8- The Lord is their strength, and he is the saving strength of his anointed. 9- Save thy people, and bless thine inheritance: feed them also, and lift them up for ever.

Psalm 29

Give unto the Lord, O ye mighty, give unto the Lord glory and strength. 2- Give unto the Lord the glory due unto his name; worship the Lord in the beauty of holiness. 3- The voice of the Lord is upon the waters: the God of glory thundereth: the Lord is upon many waters. 4- The voice of the Lord is powerful; the voice of the Lord is full of majesty. 5- The voice of the Lord breaketh the cedars; yea, the Lord breaketh the cedars of Lebanon. 6- He maketh them also to skip like a calf; Lebanon and sirion like a young unicorn. 7- The voice of the Lord divideth the flames of fire. 8- The voice of the Lord shaketh the wilderness; the Lord shaketh the Kadesh. 9- The voice of the Lord makeh the hinds to calve, and discovereth the forests: and in his temple doth every one speak of his glory. 10- The Lord sitteth upon the floor; yea, the Lord sitteth King for ever. 11- The Lord will give strength unto his people; the Lord will bless his people with peace.

Psalm 30

I will extol thee, O LORD; for thou hast lifted me up, and hast not made my foes to rejoice over me. 2- O LORD my God, I cried unto thee, and thou hast healed me. 3- O LORD, thou hast brought up my soul from the grave: thou hast kept me alive, that I should not go down to the pit. 4- Sing unto the LORD, O ye saints of his, and give thanks at the remembrance of his holiness. 5- For his anger endureth but a moment; in his favour is life: weeping may endure for a night, but joy cometh in the morning. 6- And in my prosperity I said, I shall never be moved. 7- LORD, by thy favour thou hast made my mountain to stand strong: thou didst hide thy face, and I was troubled. 8-I cried to thee, O LORD; and unto the LORD I made supplication. 9- What profit is there in my blood, when I go down to the pit? Shall the dust praise thee? shall it declare thy truth? 10- Hear, O LORD, and have mercy upon me: LORD, be thou my helper. 11-Thou hast turned for me my mourning into dancing: thou hast put off my sackcloth, and girded me with gladness; 12- To the end that my glory may sing praise to thee, and not be silent. O LORD my God, I will give thanks unto thee for ever.

Psalm 31

In thee, O LORD, do I put my trust; let me never be ashamed: deliver me in thy righteousness. 2-Bow down thine ear to me; deliver me speedily: be thou my strong rock, for an house of defence to save me. 3- For thou art my rock and my fortress; therefore for thy name's sake lead me, and guide me. 4-Pull me out of the net that they have laid privily for me: for thou art my strength. 5- Into thine hand I commit my spirit: thou hast redeemed me, O LORD God of truth. 6- I have hated them that regard lying vanities: but I trust in the LORD. 7- I will be glad and rejoice in thy mercy: for thou hast considered my trouble; thou hast known my soul in adversities; 8- And hast not shut me up into the hand of the enemy: thou hast set my feet in a large room. 9- Have mercy upon me, O LORD, for I am in trouble: mine eye is consumed with grief, yea, my soul and my belly. 10- For my life is spent with grief, and my years with sighing: my strength faileth because of mine iniquity, and my bones are consumed. 11- I was a reproach among all mine enemies, but especially among my neighbours, and a fear to mine acquaintance: they that did see me without fled from me. 12-I am forgotten as a dead man out of mind: I am like a broken vessel. 13- For I have heard the slander of many: fear was on every side: while they took counsel together against me, they devised to take away my life. 14-But I trusted in thee, O LORD: I said, Thou art my God. 15- My times are in thy hand: deliver me from the hand of mine enemies, and from them that persecute me. 16- Make thy face to shine upon thy servant: save me for thy mercies' sake. 17- Let me not be ashamed, O LORD; for I have called upon thee: let the wicked be ashamed, and let them be silent in the grave. 18- Let the lying lips be put to silence; which speak grievous things proudly and contemptuously against the righteous. 19- Oh how great is thy goodness, which thou hast laid up for them that fear thee; which thou hast wrought for them that trust in thee before the sons of men! 20- Thou shalt hide them in the secret of thy presence from the pride of man: thou shalt keep them secretly in a pavilion from the strife of tongues. 21- Blessed be the LORD: for he hath shewed me his marvellous kindness in a strong city. 22- For I said in my haste, I am cut off from before thine eyes: nevertheless thou heardest the voice of my supplications when I cried unto thee. 23- O love the LORD, all ye his saints: for the LORD preserveth the faithful, and plentifully rewardeth the proud doer. 24- Be of good courage, and he shall strengthen your heart, all ye that hope in the LORD.

Psalm 32

Blessed is he whose transgression is forgiven, whose sin is covered. 2- Blessed is the man unto whom the LORD imputeth not iniquity, and in whose spirit there is no guile. 3- When I kept silence, my bones waxed old through my roaring all the day long. 4- For day and night thy hand was heavy upon me: my moisture is turned into the drought of summer. Selah. 5- I acknowledge my sin unto thee, and mine iniquity have I not hid. I said, I will confess my transgressions unto the LORD; and thou forgavest the iniquity of my sin. Selah. 6- For this shall every one that is godly pray unto thee in a time when thou mayest be found: surely in the floods of great waters they shall not come nigh unto him. 7- Thou art my hiding place; thou shalt preserve me from trouble; thou shalt compass me about with songs of deliverance. Selah. 8- I will instruct thee and teach thee in the way which thou shalt go: I will guide thee with mine eye. 9-Be ye not as the horse, or as the mule, which have no understanding: whose mouth must be held in with bit and bridle, lest they come near unto thee. 10- Many sorrows shall be to the wicked: but he that trusteth in the LORD, mercy shall compass him about. 11- Be glad in the LORD, and rejoice, ye righteous: and shout for joy, all ye that are upright in heart.

Psalm 34

I will bless the LORD at all times: his praise shall continually be in my mouth. 2- My soul shall make her boast in the LORD: the humble shall hear thereof, and be glad. 3-O magnify the LORD with me, and let us exalt his name together. 4-I sought the LORD, and he heard me, and delivered me from all my fears. 5- They looked unto him, and were lightened: and their faces were not ashamed. 6- This poor man cried, and the LORD heard him, and saved him out of all his troubles. 7-The angel of the LORD encampeth round about them that fear him, and delivereth them. 8- O taste and see that the LORD is good: blessed is the man that trusteth in him. 9-O fear the LORD, ye his saints: for there is no want to them that fear him. 10- The young lions do lack, and suffer hunger: but they that seek the LORD shall not want any good thing. 11- Come, ye children, hearken unto me: I will teach you the fear of the LORD. 12- What man is he that desireth life, and loveth many days, that he may see good? 13- Keep thy tongue from evil, and thy lips from speaking guile. 14- Depart from evil, and do good; seek peace, and pursue it. 15- The eyes of the LORD are upon the righteous, and his ears are open unto their cry. 16-The face of the LORD is against them that do evil, to cut off the remembrance of them from the earth. 17-The righteous cry, and the LORD heareth, and delivereth them out of all their troubles. 18-The LORD is nigh unto them that are of a broken heart; and saveth such as be of a contrite spirit. 19- Many are the afflictions of the righteous: but the LORD delivereth him out of them all. 20- He keepeth all his bones: not one of them is broken. 21-Evil shall slay the wicked: and they that hate the righteous shall be desolate. 22- The LORD redeemeth the soul of his servants: and none of them that trust in him shall be desolate.

Chapter 4
The Way of Life Lao Tzu

1.

There are ways but the Way is uncharted;
There are names but not nature in words:
Nameless indeed is the source of creation
But things have a mother and she has a name.
The secret waits for the insight
Of eyes unclouded by longing;
Those who are bound by desire
See only the outward container.
These two come paired but distinct
By their names.
Of all things profound,
Say that things pairing is deepest,
The gate to the root of the world.

4.

The Way is a void,
Used but never filled:
An abyss it is,
Like an ancestor
From which all things come.
It blunts sharpness,
Resolves tangles;
It tempers light,
Subdues turmoil.
A deep pool it is,
Never to run dry!
Whose offspring it may be
I do not know
It is like a preface to God.

6.

The valley spirit is not dead:
They say it is the mystic female.
Her gateway is, they further say,
The base of earth and heaven.
Constantly, and so forever,
Use her without labor.

7.

The sky is everlasting
And the earth is very old.
Why so? Because the world
Exists not for itself:
It can and will live on.
The Wise Man chooses to be last
And so becomes the first of all;
Denying self, he too is saved.
For does he not fulfillment find
In being an unselfish man?

8.

The highest goodness, water-like,
Does good to everything and goes
Unmurmuring to places men despise;
But so, is close in nature to the Way.
If the good of the house is from land,
Or the good of the mind is its depth,
Or love is the virtue of friendship,
Or honesty blesses one's talk.
Or in government, goodness is order,
Or in business, skill is admired,
Or the worth of an act lies in timing,
Then peace is the goal of the Way
By which no one ever goes astray.

9.

To take all you want
Is never as good
As to stop when you should.
Scheme and be sharp
And you'll not keep it long.
One never can guard
His home when it's full
Of jade and fine gold:
Wealth, power and pride
Bequeath their own doom.
When fame and success
Come to you, then retire.
This is the ordained Way.

13.
"Favor, like disgrace
Brings trouble with it;
High rank, like self,
Involves acute distress,"
What does that mean, to say
That "favor, like disgrace
Brings trouble with it"?
When favor is bestowed
On one of low degree,
Trouble will come with it.
The loss of favor too
Means trouble for that man.
This, then, is what is meant
By, "favor, like disgrace
Brings trouble with it."
What does it mean, to say
That "rank, like self,
Involves acute distress"?
I suffer most because
Of me and selfishness.
If I were selfless, then
What suffering would I bear?
In governing the world,
Let rule entrusted be
To him who treats his rank
As if it were his soul;
World sovereignty can be
Committed to that man

Who loves all people
As he loves himself.

15.

The excellent masters of old,
Subtle, mysterious, mystic, acute,
Were much too profound for their times.
Since they were not then understood,
It is better to tell how they looked.
Like men crossing streams in the winter,
       How cautious!
As if all around there were danger,
       How watchful!
As if they were guests on every occasion,
       How dignified!
Like ice just beginning to melt,
       Self-effacing!
Like a wood-block untouched by a tool,
       How sincere!
Like a valley awaiting a guest,
       How receptive!
Like a torrent that rushes along,
       And so turbid!
Who, running dirty, comes clean like still waters?
Who, being quiet, moves others to fullness of life?
It is he who, embracing the Way, is not greedy;
Who endures wear and tear without needing renewal.

22.

The crooked shall be made straight
And the rough places plain;
The pools shall be filled
And the worn renewed;
The needy shall receive
And the rich shall be perplexed.
So the Wise man cherishes the One,
As a standard to the world:
Not displaying himself,
He is famous;
Not asserting himself,
He is distinguished;
Not boasting his powers,
He is effective;
Taking no pride in himself,
He is chief.
Because he is no competitor,
No one in all the world
Can compete with him.
The saying of the men of old
Is not in vain:
"The crooked shall be made straight-"
To be perfect, return to it.

25.

Something there is, whose veiled creation was
Before the earth or sky began to be;
So silent, so aloof and so alone,
It changes not, nor fails, but touches all:
Conceive it as the mother of the world.
I do not know its name;
A name for it is "Way";
Pressed for designation,
I call it Great.
Great means outgoing,
Outgoing, far-reaching,
Far-reaching, return.
The Way is great,
The sky is great,
The earth is great,
The king also is great.
Within the realm
These four are great;
The king but stands
For one of them.
Man conforms to the earth;
The earth conforms to the sky;
The sky conforms to the Way;
The Way conforms to its own nature.

33.

It is wisdom to know others;

It is enlightenment to know one's self.

The conqueror of men is powerful;

The master of himself is strong.

It is wealth to be content;

It is willful to force one's way on others.

Endurance is to keep one's place;

Long life it is die and not perish.

42.

The Way begot one,
And the one, two;
Then the two begot three
And three, all else.
All things bear the shade on their backs
And the sun in their arms;
By the blending of breath
From the sun and the shade,
Equilibrium comes to the world.
Orphaned, or needy, or desolate, these
Are conditions much feared and disliked:
Yet in public address, the king
And the nobles account themselves thus.
So a loss sometimes benefit one
Or a benefit proves to be loss.
What others have taught
I also shall teach:
If a violent man does not come
To a violent death,
I shall choose him to teach me.

43.

The softest of stuff in the world
Penetrates quickly the hardest;
Insubstantial, it enters
Where no room is.
By this I know the benefit
Of something done by quiet being;
In all the world but few can know
Accomplishment apart from work,
Instruction when no words are used.

44.

Which is dearer, fame or self?
Which is worth more, man or pelf?
Which would hurt more, gain or loss?
The mean man pays the highest prices;
The hoarder takes the greatest loss;
A men content is never shamed,
And self-restrained is not in danger:
He will live forever.

45.

Most perfect, yet it seems
Imperfect, incomplete:
Its use is not impaired.
Filled up, and yet it seems
Poured out, an empty void:
It never will run dry.
The straightest, yet it seems
To deviate, to bend;
The highest skill and yet
It looks like clumsiness.
The utmost eloquence,
It sounds like stammering.
As movement overcomes
The cold, and stillness, heat,
The Wise Man, pure and still,
Will rectify the world.

47.

The world may be known
Without leaving the house;
The Way may be seen
 Apart from the windows.
The further you go,
The less you will know.
Accordingly, the Wise Man
Knows without going,
Sees without seeing,
Does without doing.

48.

The student learns by daily increment.
The Way is gained by daily loss,
Loss upon loss until
At last comes rest.
By letting go, it all gets done;
The world is won by those who let it go!
But when you try and try,
The worlds is then beyond the winning.

56.

Those who know do not talk
And talkers do not know.

Stop your senses,
Close the doors;
Let sharp things be blunted,
Tangles resolved,
The light tempered
And turmoil subdued;
For this is mystic unity
In which the Wise Man is moved
Neither by affection
Nor yet by estrangement
Or profit or loss
Or honor or shame.
Accordingly, by all the world,
He is held highest.

Afterword
How to Elevate a Relative

Elevating a Relative

How to help a relative who took their own life or died an accidental/violent death. Sometimes the dead will cry for help, hence the need for elevation.

One way to help elevate a relative through prayer is to do the following: 9 church masses, 9 days of rosaries. Then pray/meditate to try to access where they are in their stage of elevation.

If you feel that further elevation is needed, then do 9 days of prayers with the 9 bricks next to the boveda lifting the water and new candle on each brick as one in placed on top of the other day by day. The litany of the dead prayer must be read every day as part of the list of prayers for elevation.

What we do not complete in the land of the living, we must complete in the land of the dead.

This is not done only for suicide victims and victims of violent or accidental deaths, but for anyone who has died dissatisfied and is still lingering on earth with no light. This state brings bad luck and lack of prosperity to their family.

References

Lao-tzu., & Blakney, R. B. (1955). *The way of life*. New York: New American Library.

LoyolaPress.Com, (2013) Traditional Catholic Prayers - A Jesuit Ministry Retrieved from http://www.loyolapress.com/traditional-catholic-prayers.htm

New Testament Book of Psalm Bible Press International

Vermès, G. (1997). The complete Dead Sea scrolls in English. New York, N.Y.: Allen Lane/Penguin Press.